THE BULGE OF AFRICA

THE BULGE OF AFRICA

SENEGAL, GUINEA, IVORY COAST, TOGO, BENIN, AND EQUATORIAL GUINEA

BY GEORGE S. FICHTER

FRANKLIN WATTS
New York | London | Toronto | Sydney | 1981
A FIRST BOOK

A GROLIER COMPANY

Photographs courtesy of:
Wide World Photos: pp. 23, 27;
WHO by M. Jacot: p. 15;
Bernard P. Wolff/Photo Researchers, Inc.: p. 34;
John Elk III/Bruce Coleman, Inc.: p. 37;
United Nations: pp. 45 (B. Wolff), 54.

Maps courtesy of Vantage Art, Inc.

Library of Congress Cataloging in Publication Data

Fichter, George S
The bulge of Africa.

(A First book)
Bibliography: p.
Includes index.
SUMMARY: A brief look at the history, geography,
culture, and present-day events and conditions in the
six countries located in the western bulge of Africa.
1. Africa, French-speaking West—Juvenile literature.
2. Equatorial Guinea—Juvenile literature. [1. Africa,
French-speaking West. 2. Equatorial Guinea]
I. Title.
DT524.F52   966   80–25550
ISBN 0–531–04270–7

CONTENTS

THE BULGE
OF AFRICA

Africa

1

AFRICA—THEN
AND NOW

The western coast of the immense continent of Africa bulges far into the Atlantic Ocean, its underside close to the equator. Most of this hump's southern shores are low, with lagoons and mangrove swamps that give way to steamy jungles. Farther inland, the land rises to grassy plateaus and, in a few places, mountainous highlands. The land then slopes downward again, first into bush and grass country, the savannahs, and finally into the broad, sandy bowl of the great Sahara Desert. It was along the coast of the Gulf of Guinea, the tropical underbelly of the bulge, where in the 1400s European explorers first penetrated the Dark Continent.

The Europeans were not the first humans in this part of Africa, however. Based on what we know now, the beginning of all human life on earth took place in Africa. Beginning on this continent, humans spread to other land areas of the world. Over the many centuries, those living on the continent of Africa became divided into hundreds of small groups and tribes.

But while the rest of the world strode forward, Africa stayed with its past. Isolated from the mainstream of civilization, the people there managed to survive against the odds of wild animals, diseases, torrential rains, a searing sun, and other hostile conditions that made living far from comfortable.

Compared to cultures that developed in other parts of the world, most of the Africans remained primitive. But they did have powerful organizations. Long before the Europeans arrived, great empires existed in this part of Africa. They were ruled by tribal kings who, in the religious beliefs of these people, were also divine.

The first contact these people had with the rest of the world came from across the sands of the Sahara Desert. For hundreds of years, a few trade routes existed with the Arabs, who traveled across the Sahara by camel caravan. The Arabs made the long and dangerous trip carrying with them salt and other items that could be traded for gold. And it was the source of this gold that the Europeans determined to find. The Muslims who controlled northern Africa would not allow them to journey across the Sahara to do their exploring, and so they set out to sea to sail around the big desert.

EXPLORERS AND EXPLOITERS

The western coast of Africa was not easy to sail. The big bulge is smooth, and so its coast offered almost no place where a ship could put in to escape stormy seas or even to drop anchor for going ashore to explore. Further, the winds along the coast blow consistently from the north. This made going south very easy, but it meant returning against the wind.

By 1446, the expert Portuguese seamen had sailed the African coast south to what is now Senegal. By 1472, their ships appeared regularly in the Gulf of Guinea, and in some places they already had begun to build stone castle fortresses. They were not alone. Now British, French, Spanish, Dutch, and ships of other countries plied the coastal waters. All were seeking the riches they believed to be bountiful in this mysterious land.

Some ships carried cargoes of items for trading with the Africans. The cargoes they carried home were far more valuable than what they brought, of course, for they took back with them gold, diamonds, ivory, gum arabic, ostrich feathers, and pepper. At first the Europeans treated the tribal leaders with great respect, for they found them to be clever traders. The trades were not really fair, but at least there was an exchange with a gain on both sides. The bartering was one-sided only in terms of what each wanted. No one was dissatisfied.

THE SLAVE TRADE

Slavery existed in Africa long before the arrival of the Europeans. Tribes regularly fought each other, and those who were taken prisoner in war were forced to work for their captors. In most cases, these slaves could eventually earn their freedom by work and good behavior. They also became free if they married a member of the tribe that had captured them.

Because they were familiar with slavery of this sort, the tribal chiefs did not hesitate to sell captives to the Europeans. In the beginning, only a few were sold. But for the Europeans, this new commodity was soon to become far more valuable than the gold, diamonds, and ivory they had sought originally.

Ship after ship came to the coast to be filled with human cargo destined for the American colonies where the slaves became beasts of burden. Many were literally worked to death, but these losses were quickly replaced with new purchases. The slave traders demanded more and more, the drain becoming increasingly great on the tribes. In the very early years, the Portuguese alone were said to have carried away more than a million slaves. Before the slave trade ended nearly four hundred years later, the total number of slaves sold to the Americas is believed to have reached at least 15 million. Perhaps as many millions died in the raids to capture them in Africa or of starvation and disease before ever reaching the market.

It was the discovery of America that provided the big market for slaves. Ships sailed from Europe to West Africa carrying cargoes of fabrics and other items to sell to the tribal chiefs. They took as pay as many captives or "slaves" as their ships could hold. In America, these cargoes of humans brought a big price. Then the ships were loaded with tobacco, sugar, and other products to take back to Europe. It was a profitable business. The steady demands for products contributed to the Industrial Revolution in Europe, where machinery was taking the place of human power. In the Americas it was the slave power that helped produce the bountiful crops.

The Africans themselves participated actively and eagerly in the slave trade. The tribal chiefs cultivated a dependency on products that could be bought from the Europeans with only one export—slaves. Thus the chiefs literally trapped themselves. The tribes fought each other constantly to collect more humans for export, and they were, of course, encouraged to do so by the Europeans. It was a vicious circle. To be powerful, either for protection or for aggression, the Africans needed guns. They could buy them only by selling more slaves.

Starting with England in 1807, the European countries began to ban slave trade. The slackening came only gradually though. In the United States, for example, slavery was continued until the Civil War, and it was not stopped in other parts of the world until even later. But the result was the same. The Europeans emerged powerful, and the African nations were made weak, disorganized, and distrustful even of each other.

COLONIALISM

In 1885, the countries of Europe decided that the time had come to divide Africa, each to lay claim by conquest to particular blocks of land that cut the continent into jigsaw pieces. With their armies, they marched across the continent to confirm their ownership of these parcels. Now they were no longer concerned only with the coast but also with the continent's unexplored interior. They were, by their explanation, "opening up" and bringing civilization to the Dark Continent. The era of colonialism in Africa thus began.

Under colonial rule, the countries were exploited for their natural resources—timber, gems, gold, and other valuable metals and ores. The Africans were paid for their labor but, with few exceptions, only poorly and then taxed so heavily that what they earned had to be given back almost immediately to the government. As individuals or as a people, the Africans had little opportunity to advance themselves. Rarely were the Africans treated as equals. Rather, they were still considered to be near-wild, childlike savages. For the Africans, this was only a slight change from slavery.

FERMENT FOR FREEDOM

Through Christian missionaries and by similar means, the Africans were learning about the modern world. Some began to chant for freedom. By the mid-1900s, if it were not granted outright, they began to fight for it. Slowly, and in some cases only after bloody conflicts ranging from minor skirmishes to all-out wars, the demands of the Africans began to be met. The huge colonial empires were divided into independent countries.

The Africans began a new life with a new freedom under new flags. Some were well prepared for this independence; others were not. And so the ferment and in some places turmoil continue, the young countries still unsettled and still adjusting to their new freedom. Their course has been charted, however, and they will find their way. Now all that is needed is stability and maturity. A quarter of a century is, after all, only a brief time in this land of ultimate contrasts. Africa's long history includes all that is known of the beginnings of human life and civilization and yet today it still has the youngest and most struggling of the world's nations.

Four of the countries—Senegal, Guinea, Benin, and Ivory Coast—were once a part of French West Africa. Togo was first a German colony, but its rule was granted to the French and British after World War I. Equatorial Guinea was originally a Spanish colony. All of these countries have coastal frontage, Senegal and Guinea directly on the Atlantic and the others on the Gulf of Guinea. Each country is different, and yet because they are close geographically and most have similar tribal backgrounds, the people and their ways of life are much alike.

THE PEOPLE TODAY
Today the people in these countries of Africa are at a crossroads. Their ways of life show extreme contrasts.

Some of the people—but only a small percentage—are edu-

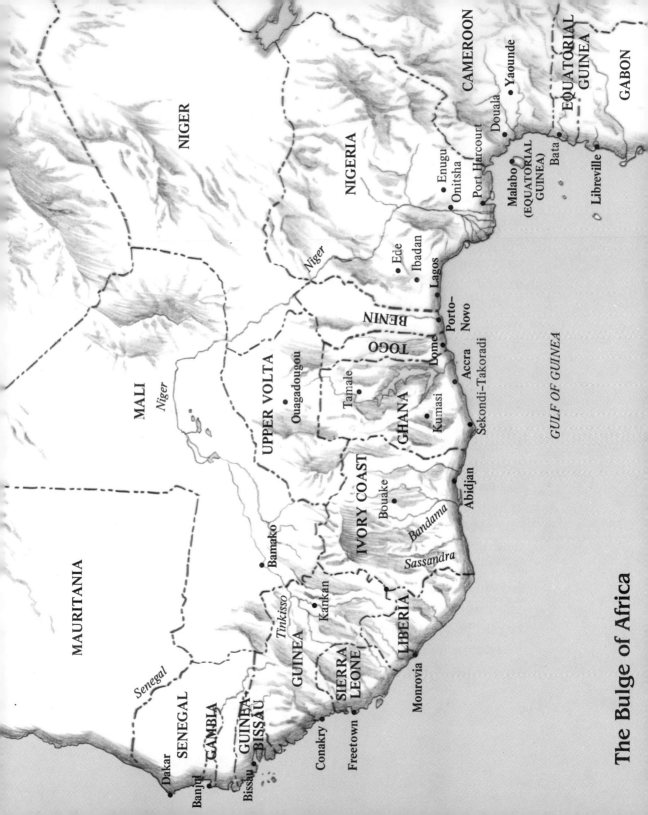

MAURITANIA

MALI

NIGER

SENEGAL

Senegal

Dakar

Banjul

GAMBIA

GUINEA-BISSAU

Bissau

GUINEA

Conakry

Freetown

SIERRA LEONE

Tinkisso

Kankan

Niger

Bamako

UPPER VOLTA

Ouagadougou

Tamale

Niger

LIBERIA

Monrovia

IVORY COAST

Bouake

Bandama

Sassandra

Abidjan

GHANA

Kumasi

Sekondi-Takoradi

Accra

Lome

TOGO

BENIN

Porto-Novo

Lagos

Ede

Ibadan

NIGERIA

Enugu

Onitsha

Port Harcourt

Douala

CAMEROON

Yaounde

EQUATORIAL GUINEA

Malabo (EQUATORIAL GUINEA)

Bata

GABON

Libreville

GULF OF GUINEA

The Bulge of Africa

cated and completely modernized in their ways of thinking and living. Others cling to the old patterns. It is not a matter of declaring one way right, the other wrong. The problem, rather, is in bringing the two together to achieve comfortable and harmonious solutions for everyone.

If you were to visit the big cities in these countries, you would find them bustling centers of business with modern office buildings, hotels and apartments, shops and department stores, restaurants and theaters, parks, flashing traffic signals, automobiles creeping bumper to bumper—not unlike cities elsewhere in the world, with all their conveniences and trappings. You would find the well-to-do in tree-shaded residential suburbs, and the very poor in ghettolike slums.

But within perhaps a mile of the metropolises, people may still live in hovels in the bush, almost as primitive in ways of life as their ancestors. These are people who live with and as a part of nature day by day. These are the people who gave rise to the legends of Africa. True, the city people are really no less dependent on nature for their survival, but they do not work with it directly and are much less aware of their natural world. Theirs is more a world of people.

The old Africa was thousands of years in existence before it was invaded by people from other parts of the world. Except for its fringes, remember, much of the continent has been known for only slightly more than a century. All of the major advances and inventions had passed the Africans by. Until the Europeans began their settlements there, as just one example, the Africans had not seen the wheel.

Some of the changes thrust at these people have come too

quickly for acceptance. But there is good to be said for at least some of their tribal customs. In the old days, people felt secure in belonging to a tribe. The tribe was their extended family. The whole tribe prospered or failed. The spoils were shared. The carry-over of this "big family" custom into modern cultures that stress the individual has been a major problem. According to old tribal ways, an African who works and is paid money is expected to share. But the amount of work is limited, and so the labor of one individual is commonly spread over many. The individual worker is unable to accumulate or build personal resources, and everyone remains poor.

About 90 percent of the people still live on the land. A family clears a small plot of land—just enough to provide subsistence from the crops that can be grown there. When the soil is no longer fertile enough to grow crops, the plot is abandoned, and new land is cleared. Their diets consist mainly of cereal grains and starches with very little protein. This is changing, too, as the countries learn more about different kinds of farming and also about the importance of good nutrition.

Africa today, is, in effect, a battle of yesterday against today and tomorrow. But yesterday, even though it exists a mile into the country, is really gone forever. Only today and tomorrow can emerge victorious.

The Africans understandably want assurance that the independence they have gained is real and not bound by political encumbrances. They are anxious for a freedom of their own making, not one that is imposed on them by outsiders and thus not really a freedom at all. These people are struggling desperately to find their way, and so they turn eagerly toward any governmental doctrines that seem to offer the desired answer for them as individuals and as a people collectively. In this headlong plunge, they have made mistakes—but eventually they will correct them. Their search continues, and their answers will come from the Africa of today and tomorrow, the Africa of yesterday left behind forever.

2

REPUBLIC OF SENEGAL

The French made their first settlement in Black Africa at Senegal, located on Africa's extreme western bulge. But the Portuguese had made landings here even earlier.

Senegal covers some 75,750 square miles (196,192 sq km), roughly the size of the state of South Dakota. It is bounded on the north and east by the Senegal and Falémé rivers, which separate the country from Mauritania and Mali. To its south is Guinea, and curiously, it is cut into along its southern third by the tiny, pencil-like country of Gambia. Senegal fronts on the Atlantic Ocean with a 227-mile (446-km) coastline.

The southern portion of Senegal, around the Casamance River, is forested, and in the southeastern section there are mountains, the foothills of the Futa Jallons. But most of Senegal is a flat and sandy savannah, less than 300 feet (100 m) above sea level. The far northern portion is semidesert.

Though the Portuguese, British, and Dutch established colonies here very early, the French, who did not arrive until the 1500s, stayed longest and left the deepest imprint. Not surprisingly, the official language today is French, which is taught in the schools. Many Senegalese still use their tribal language, however, and of these, Wolof is the most commonly spoken.

CLIMATE
From December through May, most of Senegal is dry and warm, the temperature ranging from 66 to 85 degrees F (18 to 29 degrees C). From June through November, Senegal is hot, the temperature rarely below 80 degrees F (27 degrees C) and commonly higher. In the south, along the coast and toward the equator, the rainfall is heavy, about 80 inches (203 cm) per year; to the north and east, toward the Sahara, rainfall is slight, less than 20 inches (50 cm) in some areas.

Because of its generally pleasant weather and breezy beaches, Senegal is popular with tourists visiting West Africa.

PEOPLE
Of all the people of West Africa, the Senegalese have had the longest contact with Europeans and also with the Berbers to the north. Most of them belonged originally to the Wolof tribe, and yet today the Wolofs account for about only a third of the population. Other tribes of the region are the Fulani, Serer, and Toucouleur. In the south are the Dioula and the Malinké.

Basically, all were true Negroes, their skin brown to blue-black, with jet-black hair, flat and broad noses, and thick lips. But beginning centuries ago, and particularly among those living in the northern sections, intermarriages occurred with the Berbers. The result was a taller people with more delicate features. When these people were taken as slaves, they were frequently singled out to be house servants or to do other kinds of work that kept them out of the fields and away from the most grueling tasks. Senegalese remain to this day a very striking people and notably hospitable and kind.

Because they were contacted centuries ago by the Berbers traveling across the Sahara Desert in camel caravans, 75 percent of the nearly 6 million people living in Senegal today are Muslims. The remainder cling to old tribal beliefs, and a small percentage, concentrated primarily in the coastal cities, are Christian, mainly Roman Catholic. These are largely the some 60,000 Europeans, most of whom are French. Beginning in early times, too, the French also married Senegalese. Children of these people served in the French Revolution, and a number of Senegalese have been representatives in the French government, where they have been greatly respected.

CITIES

Almost a third of Senegal's people today live in towns or cities.

Dakar, the capital, is a modern city of nearly 800,000 people. Since colonial days, it has been the center for all of West Africa. It became—and still is—the largest port in West Africa, handling both freight and passenger traffic. Dakar also has a bustling international airport.

French authority in Dakar has been removed, of course, but throughout the city, the French influence, atmosphere, and architecture still prevail. Most of the roughly 40,000 French people of Dakar live on the high land, called the "plateau," at the tip of Cape Verde. In all of West Africa, Dakar remains the culture center, and the University of Dakar has an enrollment of more than 6000 students.

Dakar first became important in the 1600s as a slave port.

Two miles at sea is the island of Gorée where captives were held in a giant stone fortress and then loaded onto slave ships bound for America. Today those old slaveholding quarters are visited by tourists.

Saint-Louis, with a population of about 90,000, is also a port and was the first capital of Senegal. Settled by the French, the city is located on an island about 10 miles (16 km) from the mouth of the Senegal River, which is navigable by shallow-draft ships for nearly 700 miles (1120 km).

Ziguinchor has a population of about 75,000. It is located a short distance inshore on the Casamance River, which is navigable by oceangoing ships going to the city. Ziguinchor is on Senegal's southernmost boundary.

Inland cities include Kaolack, population 100,000, about 90 miles (150 km) from Dakar; Tambacounda, population about 75,000, about 250 miles (400 km) from Dakar; and Thiès, population 120,000, only a few miles northeast of Dakar.

Because Senegal was once the nucleus of all French West Africa, its network of internal transportation routes is better and more complete than in most of the new African nations. Railroads connect Dakar to Thiès, Louga, Saint-Louis, and Linguère to the north; to Djourbel, Touba, Kaolack, and Tambacounda to the east. All of these towns are also connected to Dakar by good roads, of which Senegal has approximately 8700 miles (14,000 km). The roads cross Gambia to Bignona, Kolda, Ziguinchor, and other towns in the southern section of the country.

NATURAL RESOURCES

Senegal's most valuable natural resource is its phosphate rocks. Phosphates are used in the fertilizer and chemical industries.

[14]

*A crowded village in Senegal. Note the canal at left,
built to route water through the village.*

Most of the phosphates are mined near Thiès and Tivaouane just north of Dakar.

In addition, Senegal has iron ore on the Falémé River. A new hydroelectric power dam on the Senegal River will provide the necessary energy for an economic recovery of the iron ore.

Oil prospecting off the coast near Ziguinchor also shows promise of providing productive wells.

The Republic of Senegal has recognized the importance of preserving its native plants and animals. At this time the country has three national parks: Niokolo-Kobo, Djoval, and Basse Casamance. There is also a special park for tropical plants near Dakar.

In the expansive Niokolo-Kobo park, a number of large native animals make their home. Among them are herds of duikers, hartebeests, roan antelopes, kobs, bushbucks, and other grazers. There are also red monkeys, vervets, and baboons; hyenas, jackals, and wild dogs; civets, caracals, leopards, lions, and servals; and occasionally seen are hippopotamuses, elephants, and giraffes. There are also cobras, pythons, and crocodiles; bustards, guinea fowls, and literally hundreds of other birds are found, the number swollen in winter by migrants.

AGRICULTURE

About 70 percent of the Senegalese are farmers. Their farms are mostly small, some producing only enough for the farmer's needs but others are farmed for cash crops.

The biggest crop is peanuts (groundnuts). In a good season, nearly a million tons of peanuts are sold by the Senegalese. But unfortunately there are also drought years when the production is less than half that amount. About 75 percent of Senegal's exports are peanuts, and so a poor peanut crop is a real disaster for the country.

Until recently the peanut was believed to be a native of Africa. Now it is known that the peanut came originally from South America, probably Peru, and was cultivated by the Indians of Central America and Mexico long before the arrival of the Spanish explorers. The peanut was introduced to Africa sometime after 1500, during the slave-trading era, and became popular there immediately. It traveled back to America with the slaves, and in those early days, peanuts were considered as worthy food only for the blacks. It was not until after the Civil War in the United States that the peanut became generally accepted by everyone. As a world trade item, in fact, peanuts were first introduced by the French from their African colonies.

Peanuts are indeed unusual plants, different enough in their growing habits to appeal to the superstitious Africans, while at the same time providing them with an easily grown and substantial food. When the flowers of a peanut plant are fertilized, they develop into heavy "pegs" that pull the branches of the plant down. As soon as the "pegs" reach the soil, they grow into it, there forming the pods containing the peanuts. This is the only plant in which the fruit actually develops and matures underground, making the name groundnut perfectly understandable.

Rice is also a staple of Senegal, though it is not produced in large enough amounts for export. About a third of the rice is grown on flooded lands around the Casamance River, the remainder in scattered floodplains of the Senegal and Falémé rivers. Corn (maize), millet, and sorghum are other important field crops and are commonly rotated with peanuts. In the grasslands, the Senegalese keep big herds of cattle, and in the southwest, there are sheep and goats in the hill country. Nearly every farm and village has many chickens.

Senegal has been slow in developing new crops to avoid its great dependency on peanuts as a source of income, but a succession of droughts in recent years has made it evident that diversification is essential. Cotton, for example, is one of the newer crops now being grown in greater amounts, and it is helping to change the agricultural pattern.

INDUSTRY

Senegal is the most industrialized of the countries that once formed French West Africa. It now has a number of food-processing plants. These include fish, peanuts, sugar refineries, flour mills, and others. There are also fertilizer, soap, plywood, and other industries, the number and different kinds increasing regularly.

Senegalese officials are trying to smooth out their economy so that the income from exports equals what they must spend for imports. Industries are essential to prevent their total reliance on agriculture.

The largest new enterprise is an oil refinery and chemical complex just north of Dakar, the installation funded partly by Iran. Close to the source of phosphates, the huge complex can not only refine oil but also manufacture fertilizer, plastics, and other synthetics.

GOVERNMENT

As an independent nation, Senegal elects a president and a National Assembly every five years. So far, the president has been Léopold-Sédar Senghor. A longtime politician, President Senghor is an influential, polished, and skilled statesman. He has a good working relationship with France and other Western nations.

President Senghor has been criticized for squelching attempts to organize opposing parties. He has stated, however, that he will welcome opposition from acceptable, nonradical groups, and that when these groups are indeed representative of his country and its needs, he will resign, his task accomplished.

3

REPUBLIC OF
GUINEA

Guinea is the most beautiful of all the old French West Africa
countries. From its mangrove-fringed tropical coast on the
Atlantic, it ranges to savannahs and then mountains in the east.
But much of the inland area is a rolling plain, about 1000 feet
(300 m) above sea level. The country's highest peak is 5575-
foot (1732-m) Mount Nimba in the southwest on the border of
the Ivory Coast, and in Guinea's Futa Jallon Mountains the
Niger, Senegal, and Gambia rivers are born.

Guinea is bounded to the south by Liberia and Sierra
Leone; to the north and west by Senegal and Mali; to the east
by the Ivory Coast. Its size is 94,926 square miles (245,857 sq
km), or only slightly smaller than the state of Wyoming.

In ancient times Guinea was a part of the huge Ghana empire that dominated most of western Africa south of the Sahara.
Later, in the 1200s, it became part of the Malinké empire and remained so for some four centuries. It was during this time that

the Europeans arrived off the Guinea coast, first the Portuguese in the 1400s and soon afterward the British and the French. Guinea was never prominent in the slave trade that was active in most of the coast regions, primarily because it offered no good natural port.

In 1849, Guinea became a French territory, but the people of Guinea did not submit easily or quickly to French domination. Almary Samory Touré, best known as Chief Samory, fought the French in bitter and bloody battles for sixteen years before he was finally captured. The nation's present leader, President Sékou Touré, is Chief Samory's grandson.

CLIMATE

Located near the equator, Guinea's tropical coast is always hot and humid. It has a dry season from about November until at least mid-May in most of the country, but during the summer and fall, the rains are heavy. At Conakry, the capital, about 168 inches (430 cm) of rain falls annually, more than half of it in July and August. In torrential downpours, a person can see for only a short distance. The temperature ranges from a winter low of 60 degrees F (15 degrees C) to a summer high of about 100 degrees F (37 degrees C).

PEOPLE

Because Guinea was a French colony for many years, the language used in official documents today is still French, and French is still taught in the schools. But only a small percentage of the nation's more than 5 million people speak French. They are mostly the Europeans who live in or near Conakry or in one of the mining towns. Most Guineans are members of the Malinké,

Susu, Fulani, or other tribal groups, and they speak their native languages. The present Guinean government intends to eliminate French eventually in favor of one or more of these traditional local languages. Guinea has more than 2000 schools, but fewer than half of the children attend. The literacy rate in Guinea is still low.

Influenced by visits from the Berbers from the north centuries ago, about 65 percent of the Guineans are Muslims, and they often combine their Islamic belief with their tribal religion. Only a small percentage of Guineans are Christians.

Conakry, its incity population about 200,000 but with another 250,000 living in the immediate vicinity, is Guinea's busy capital. Conakry also has a large deepwater port. A railroad connects Conakry to Kindia, Dabola, and Kankan, the railroad's terminal point in Upper Guinea. There is also a railroad to Fria, about 50 miles (80 km) northeast of Conakry. Totally, the nation has nearly 500 miles (800 km) of railroads.

A nearly 5000-mile (8000-km) network of roads connects Conakry to towns and cities throughout the nation. At Conakry, too, there is an international airport plus airline connections to smaller cities throughout the country.

NATURAL RESOURCES

Guinea's valuable natural resources include exceptionally large deposits of bauxite (an aluminum ore) and iron. The foothills north of Macenta yield about 80 carats of diamonds annually, and there are also substantial gold deposits in the hill country.

Exploitation of the bauxite began after World War II, and the country now produces about 80 percent of all the bauxite mined in Africa. It is estimated by some authorities that Guinea

*A Guinean mother and her children gather
outside their thatched roof home.*

has 20 percent of the world's bauxite, which makes this small country very rich indeed.

Several other countries are heavily involved in the mining operations. These include the Soviet Union, Yugoslavia, Switzerland, several Arab nations, and others. To handle the large amounts of ore from the Sangredi mine in the western portion of the country, a new port was built at Kamsar. The Sangredi mine is expected to be producing 30 million tons of bauxite annually by the mid-1980s. In 1972, by comparison, the total output for all of Guinea was only a little more than 2½ million tons.

Guinea's iron ore is located in the southeastern area of the country, most of it near and on Mount Nimba. The mining there poses a grave threat to the national park, but Guinea is nevertheless moving ahead with construction of a railroad from Mount Nimba to the port at Conakry for hauling the ore. Investments in the iron mining project have come from iron and steel companies in France and also from several countries in Africa.

Three-fourths of the Mount Nimba Reserve lies in Guinea, and because the nation does not at this time have any other area in which its native plants and animals are protected, conservationists throughout the world worry about the destruction of this irreplaceable natural resource. The conservationists, in fact, have worked to enlarge the reserve. They would like to see it extended southward into Liberia, an area also rich in iron ore.

Many kinds of native African animals live in the reserve. It is true that most of them are found in other parts of Africa, too, but with the continent's increasing development, all are greatly reduced in numbers and forced now to exist in shrunken ranges. Some are extremely rare. To biologists, the Mount

Nimba Reserve is famous for a small toad that bears its young alive. The toad has no other living relatives closer than 3000 miles (4800 km). Mount Nimba is unique, too, for its highland savannahs—above the rain forests and the misty cloud line at about 2600 feet (800 m).

AGRICULTURE

Despite the big shift toward mining and industry to help its economy, 90 percent of the Guineans still depend on agriculture. Much of the farming is strictly for self-subsistence, but some farms produce cash crops for export. First is cassava, a plant with an edible root, the amount shipped from Guinea approaching 450,000 tons per year. The country's lowlands also produce almost as much rice, also exported. Corn (maize), bananas, palm kernels, pineapples, and coffee are other crops that are shipped. Of these, only the palm kernels come from a native plant. The rice came originally from the Far East, and the others were introduced directly or indirectly from the Americas.

The waters off Guinea's shores are rich with fish and shellfish, and so fishing has become one of the nation's growing industries. Much of the fish is consumed locally, but tuna and shrimp are harvested in sufficient quantity for export.

Unlike Senegal, however, Guinea does not depend on one agricultural product to support its economy. Guinea has diversified its agriculture and has also balanced it with mining and other industries. Because of its streams and highlands, the nation has great potential for developing hydroelectric power. A dam on the Bafing River at Koukoutamba will be finished in the early 1980s. Two others are planned for the Konkouré River.

GOVERNMENT

Until World War II, Guinea was poor—an undeveloped French territory. Until then, the nation had literally no exports. Immediately after World War II, however, the mining of bauxite and iron was begun, and by the early 1950s, Guinea had risen to become one of France's richest territories. Led by Sékou Touré, the various tribes united and began to make demands. They demanded elimination of discrimination against blacks, and they also asked for a strong voice in controlling their country. They requested higher wages, more and better schools, and other social rights and equalities.

The French did not respond to these demands. President Charles de Gaulle of France made a visit to Guinea to try to squelch the social revolution. He made various compromising offers, including self-government under the newly formed French Community. All of his offers were rejected.

"We prefer poverty in liberty to riches in slavery," Sékou Touré announced proudly in 1958. In a vote held shortly afterward, 95 percent of the Guineans echoed Touré's sentiments. The Guineans were granted freedom to become a wholly independent nation.

As in other African nations, women in Guinea are slowly progressing toward equality with men. This woman is handling a television camera during the 1978 visit of a foreign head of state.

The French were unhappy about the outcome. Some believed that the Guineans were far from experienced enough to succeed as an independent nation. Others were disturbed because they thought the Guineans were ungrateful for all that had been done for them. Still others saw the loss of Guinea as a tremendous financial disaster to France because of the investments made in the African nation's newfound riches. No matter what the reasons, the French left Guinea, and as they did, they took with them all of their movable trappings, even ripping the telephones from the walls. The French fully expected Guinea to collapse as a nation in a very short time, and their opinion was shared by many throughout the world.

Other African nations and the whole world watched with interest as Guinea began its struggle. Times were extremely difficult at first and are not wholly smoothed yet. Smuggling of items to be sold in the Ivory Coast and Sierra Leone was a major problem, for in those countries money was—and still is—more stabilized than is the still feeble value of the Guinean currency, the styli, on the world market. But the nation nevertheless survived without French help, financial or otherwise. Though the country is still not secure, the Guineans are justly proud of what they have accomplished on their own.

Since achieving independence, Guinea has been ruled by President Sékou Touré and the Guinea Democratic Party, working with a 150-member Legislative Assembly. At the start, Guinea was isolated not only from France, with considerable bitterness between the two, but also from most neighboring African nations. This made the new country's struggles all the more difficult. Now those relationships are reestablished, an immense help to Guinea in gaining its economic footing. And the Guineans, under President Touré's leadership, are in turn rallying other people of Africa to follow their path to what they describe as democratic freedom. But the truth is that the government still exerts almost complete control over the country's economy and its politics. This is not the sort of democratic freedom to which most Africans aspire.

4

REPUBLIC OF IVORY COAST

More than 325 miles (523 km) of the Ivory Coast fronts on the Gulf of Guinea. To the east the coast is low and sandy, with many lagoons. From about Grand-Lahou westward, it is rocky.

European traders came to the low coastal area in the early days to load their ships with cargoes of ivory. In those days elephants were abundant in the forest and bush country, and the huge curved tusks of big bull elephants could weigh as much as 200 pounds (90 kg) each. Though the price paid for the tusks in Africa was small, their value in the markets in Europe was great. But the price paid by the elephants themselves—their lives—was the greatest of all. Few remain today. It was nevertheless the tusks of the elephant that gave this coast its name.

Almost square in shape, the Ivory Coast covers 124,504 square miles (322,463 sq km), about the size of the state of New Mexico. The southern half of the country is a densely forested coastal plain and tropical jungle, but the land slopes up-

[30]

ward to the north, becoming a savannah, with bushes and grasses and almost no trees. In the extreme west are mountains, an extension of the Guinea highlands. Highest is Mount Nimba at 5575 feet (1732 m), standing where the Ivory Coast, Guinea, and Liberia meet. Next tallest at 4260 feet (1278 m) is Mount Tonkoui, near Man.

Three rivers—Comoe, Bandama, and Sassandra—flow from the highlands to the coast, but they are navigable only by small boats. A huge dam on the Bandama near Yamoussoukro has since 1972 produced half of the country's power. About 1 mile (1.6 km) long and 200 feet (60 m) high, the dam forms a huge lake that floods an area in which more than 75,000 people once lived. With the help of the United Nations, the people were moved to new homes and villages, all of them benefiting from the power supplied by the hydroelectric power plant. Another and even larger dam is being constructed at Bugo on the Sassandra River, and a third is being built on the Bandama River at Taoln.

CLIMATE

The southern half of the Ivory Coast is tropical, its year-round temperature 80 degrees F (27 degrees C) or higher. Rainfall is heavy, often torrential. It averages 80 inches (200 cm) per year, in some places more. Most of the rain comes between May and July, with lighter rains between October and November.

In the higher northern half of the country, the rains extend over the period from May through October, but the average fall is considerably less—50 inches (127 cm). Some areas are semidesert, with a rainfall as low as 20 inches (50 cm). The temperature also fluctuates between 60 and 80 degrees F (14 and 27 degrees C).

PEOPLE

Officially the language of the Ivory Coast is French, but many native languages are spoken by the country's 7½ million inhabitants. Among the most common languages are Senoufo, Agni, Dioula, and Baoule, for long before the arrival of the French, about 60 different tribes lived in the region. Each had its own language and customs. Because of their varied backgrounds and cultural heritage, it was at first difficult for the people of the Ivory Coast to work together as a nation. Now, more than two decades after attaining their independence, the people have at last begun to think of themselves as Ivorians first and secondly as members of their old tribes. This sort of solidarity is essential in making a new nation successful.

Among the tribes in the eastern Ivory Coast area are the Agni, Baoule, and Ebrie. Of these the Agni still have the strongest ties to their own heritage. The Baoule are well known as excellent farmers, and the Ebrie are one of several groups that build their homes on stilts over lagoon waters and live mainly by fishing.

In the dense forests and mountains to the west are the Dan (Yacouba), Wobe, Guéré, and Bete, some of whom still cling to old tribal customs. In the savannahs of the north are the Senoufo, actually formed of a group of tribes. They live mainly by farming and also persist in the old ways.

Ivory Coast's largest single group is the Dioula, who number more than a million. Though their ancestral home is in the country's northwestern section, the Dioula have since scattered over most of the area. Among the Ivorian natives, they are generally considered to be the most enterprising.

People from Benin, Togo, Guinea, and other nearby countries come to the rapidly growing and more prosperous Ivory Coast to find work. Only about 50,000 Europeans, most of them French, live in the country, and nearly all are in either Abidjan or Boule.

About 60 percent of the Ivorians practice their tribal religions, which are based on the belief that spirits occupy all objects, both living and nonliving. Some of these spirits are helpful, others harmful. A chief, or priest, keeps his people in harmony with the spirits with a combination of magic and ritual. Each tribe accomplishes this in a slightly different way.

Nearly a fourth of the Ivorians are Muslims. Introduced to West Africa by the Berbers nearly a thousand years ago, the Muslim religion blends well with traditional beliefs. Fewer than 15 percent of the Ivorians are Christians, most of them living in the southern cities. Africans have great difficulty accepting Christianity because it requires giving up all of their traditional beliefs.

More than half a million students are now enrolled in the young nation's 2000 public schools, which are patterned after the schools in France. Thousands of young adults now attend trade schools, and those who want still higher education can attend the new University of Abidjan. A daily newspaper, three weekly newspapers, eight radio stations, four television stations—these, too, help to educate the people as well as to keep them informed. They aid in bringing Ivorians together as one people. Illiteracy is still widespread in the country, but it is being eliminated steadily.

Like many Africans, the Ivorians enjoy singing and dancing. Their unique rhythms are followed to the beat of drums. The native drums are hollowed cylinders of wood covered with

hide drawn tight to make the head. Some consist only of hollowed wood. Another native instrument that is widely used in West Africa is the balafon, a xylophone made with strips of wood for keys and with gourds strapped under them to provide the resonance. In local and spontaneous song and dance sessions, everybody joins in. Some of the dances are rooted in tribal ceremony, and the performers wear special costumes and masks. The more sophisticated modern musicians playing in nightclubs and other public places in cities also use modern drums, horns, and stringed instruments, including electronic amplifiers. But the Afro beat still comes through and has been picked up by other young musicians throughout the world.

Ivorians are world renowned for their wood carving. In days gone by, most of these carvings of statues, masks, and other objects were made only for ceremonies and rituals. Now many are carved for sale to tourists or simply for the personal pleasure of the artists in expressing themselves. Some native craftspeople are also skilled at working with gold and pottery, and still others are accomplished painters. An increasing number are turning to literature, the theater, and other arts to which they have been exposed through education.

CITIES

Most Ivorians live in the country or in small villages. Only a few cities have populations of 50,000 or more.

A mosque in Abidjan, the capital of the Ivory Coast. Almost one-quarter of all Ivorians are Muslims.

Abidjan, the capital, has a population of more than 500,000, its growth from a village of fewer than a thousand taking place in only about seventy-five years. Raucous and bustling, Abidjan is a "boom" town in every sense of the word. It includes modern office buildings, luxury hotels, and other extravagant evidences of the country's phenomenal growth. Among the show places are the Ivoire Hotel and the Presidential Palace, which cost more than $10 million to build. But modern skyscrapers are now appearing regularly. Typical of quick-growth cities too, Abidjan has its share of slums, vices, and sanitary problems.

Abidjan is not only the seat of government of the Ivory Coast but also the hub for the entire country's industry, communications, shipping, and business. Nearby Bingerville, now virtually a suburb of the rapidly growing Abidjan, was the nation's first capital, but the change came in the early 1950s when a deepwater channel, the Vridi Canal, connected Abidjan to the sea and converted the city into a busy international seaport. There is now an international airport at Port-Bouët, only 10 miles (16 km) from Abidjan. A railroad runs north from Abidjan to Ferkéssédougou and on northward into Upper Volta. The 20,000-mile (32,000-km) network of roads that crosshatch the country are also focused on Abidjan.

Bouaké, its population only slightly more than 100,000, is 245 miles (392 km) directly north of Abidjan on the edge of the savannah. With space still not at a premium, Bouaké has sprawled rather than developed skyscrapers. Here is the nation's largest textile factory plus industries producing soaps, chemicals, and other products. One of the most striking structures in this city is a magnificent Muslim mosque.

Man, with a population of less than 50,000, is located in

*Abidjan is a bustling and fast-growing city,
complete with skyscrapers and suburbs.*

the mountains near the borders of Guinea and Liberia. Of the cities in the Ivory Coast, Man is the most picturesque, and a growing number of tourists go there to enjoy the city's cooler climate and its colorful folklore.

Other cities include Gagnoa, Dimbokro, Aboisso, Sassandra, Bondoukou, Odienné, Séguéla, Tabou, Daloa, and Agboville. The Democratic Party of the Ivory Coast assembles in a special building at Yamoussoukro near the Kossou Dam. On a large, government-managed plantation there, crops are grown experimentally to improve old kinds and to try new ones.

NATURAL RESOURCES

Elephants still live in Ivory Coast's forest and bush country, but they are now rare. In the sluggish rivers, hippos bathe in companionship with crocodiles. Hyenas howl and monkeys chatter. In the treetops, there are parrots and other colorful tropical birds. On the savannahs, there are fleet antelopes, lions, and leopards. But as in every country where growth is rapid, the native wildlife is giving way to civilization. Once impenetrable jungles, in which some 500 species of trees grow, are being leveled to make space for fields for crops and for roads and buildings.

Fortunately, a few wise people long ago recognized that at least some areas of our plundered planet must be preserved. The Ivory Coast thus shares with Guinea and Liberia the 45,000-acre (18,000-ha) Mount Nimba Reserve. Only about a fourth of this reserve is in the Ivory Coast. The mountain offers a unique mixture of misty rain forests and savannah habitats, providing sanctuary for chimpanzees, pygmy hippos, forest buffaloes, bongos, duikers, bushbucks, chevrotains, tree hyraxes, and many other creatures as well as plants. As a reserve, the Mount Nimba retreat excludes visitors, the tract belonging exclusively to the creatures and to the plants. Mount Nimba is rich in iron ore, however, and so it has been difficult for conservationists to prevent exploiters from destroying the preserve.

Meanwhile, steps are being taken by Ivory Coast officials to create other such areas. One, the 2½-million-acre (900,000-ha) Bouna Reserve, is open to visitors part of the year.

Native plants and animals are the Ivory Coast's greatest natural resource. Prospectors continue to search for gold and diamonds and for productive sources of iron, bauxite, and manganese. To date, however, no significant finds have been made.

AGRICULTURE

The Ivory Coast has rich soil and an abundance of water. These two extremely valuable resources have made it possible for the nation to produce not only its own food but also great amounts for export. Nearly 60 percent of the country's exports are coffee and cocoa, ranking the Ivory Coast third in the world in producing these commodities. Most of the coffee is grown on plantations of 10 acres (4 ha) or less, but the total acreage is more than a million. Other exports include pineapples and bananas. The Ivorians have diversified their crops to include rubber tree plantations, cotton, tobacco, rice, and sugar.

Palm oil, long used by the natives, is another important export item. The oil is obtained from the fruit of a native palm that is now grown on special plantations to get enough of the oil for exporting. The oil palm also yields a locally much-liked wine, called bangui. A cut is made near the top of the tree, and the sap that oozes from this wound is collected in hollow gourds. There it is allowed to ferment for several days to become wine.

Large amounts of timber are cut in the dense forests. Timber, in fact, is now the largest single export from the country, and the government's forest experts control the harvests so that the reserves are not destroyed. They have learned to treat their remaining forests as a crop. Until recently the timber was shipped only as logs, but the Ivorians are now becoming involved in processing the wood themselves—cutting and grading the logs into lumber, and also making some furniture, crates, and other finished products.

Ivorians eat well. Their principal foods are yams, plantains (a kind of banana), millet, rice, manioc (cassava), and peanuts (groundnuts). There are also mangoes, papayas, pineapples, bananas, and other tropical fruits. Foutou, the national dish of the Ivory Coast, consists of a mixture of cooked yams and plantains pounded together in a mortar to make a dough. This is eaten by dipping the fingers first into the dough and then into a meat sauce, usually highly seasoned.

Ivorians raise livestock—cattle, goats, sheep, and hogs— and they keep chickens around their dwellings for eating and for the eggs. Fish are caught along the coast. The tuna harvest is sufficiently large for exporting.

Largely due to wise agricultural practices, the Ivory Coast has in the past two decades risen from being one of the world's poorest nations to one of its most productive.

INDUSTRY

The Ivory Coast has only recently begun to industrialize. Efforts are being made, however, to use local raw materials to produce finished products for sale. In this way the Ivorians are kept employed, and the products they turn out can be used locally or exported. In either case, they command a much higher price than the raw material.

Among the new industries are an oil refinery, textile mill and clothing factory, sugar refinery, soap factory, and others. Most of the industries are located either at Abidjan or Bouaké.

GOVERNMENT

The Ivory Coast elects a president every five years, and he appoints a Council of Ministers, a 17-member advisory cabinet. There is also a National Assembly consisting of 120 members, each also serving a five-year term.

Since 1960, when the Ivory Coast became an independent nation, the Ivorians have elected Félix Houphouët-Boigny as president. A longtime and experienced champion for the cause of Africa and its people, President Houphouët-Boigny was once a member of the French National Assembly and was also prime minister of the Ivory Coast. A hero among the Ivorians and also among most other struggling African nations, the politically powerful President Houphouët-Boigny has used his influence and wisdom well on behalf of his country and can be credited with having piloted the nation on its remarkable path of progress and self-sufficiency. President Houphouët-Boigny is criticized for being more dictatorial than democratic, but he has successfully unified the dozens of tribes into a single nation and has steadfastly opposed any efforts to shred this unification.

5
REPUBLIC OF TOGO

Togo is a slim finger of land sandwiched between Ghana on its west and Benin on its east. To the north is Upper Volta. On the Gulf of Guinea, Togo's frontage is 32 miles (55 km), and the widest part of its 340-mile (547-km) length is only 90 miles (145 km). Totally, Togo contains only 21,853 square miles (35,000 sq km), making it about half the size of the state of Ohio.

The highest peak of the Atakora Mountains, which run through Togo diagonally from the northeast to the southwest, is Mount Agou, with an elevation of 3255 feet (922 m). South of the mountains the land slopes seaward to a tropical forest and then mangrove swamps and lagoons along the coast. Offshore are barrier sandbars that are becoming increasingly popular as beaches for tourist visitors. To the north are open savannahs, the land drained by the Oti River.

CLIMATE

Togo's climate is tropical—hot and humid. Its two rainy seasons are from April through July and from October through November. In December and January a cool harmattan wind blows almost constantly from the northeast. The rainfall varies—about 40 inches (100 cm) per year in the north, 70 inches (178 cm) around Klouto, but only about 30 inches (76 cm) at Lomé. The average temperature along the coast is 80 degrees F (27 degrees C). Inland, without the benefit of an ocean breeze, it is hotter, averaging 86 degrees F (30 degrees C).

PEOPLE

Most of the 2½ million people of Togo belong to one of the original tribes that inhabited the region—among them the Ewe, Cabrai, and Ouatchi. The Ewe, among the most literate of the West Africans, came into the Togo region from the Niger River Valley as long ago as the 1100s. About half of the Ewes live in neighboring Ghana, however. This splitting of tribal groups and the joining together of tribes that have in the past been competitors and enemies have caused problems in bringing Africans together as nations.

Though the official language of Togo is French, most of the people speak Ewe or other tribal languages. About 75 percent still follow their traditional tribal religions, and of the remainder, 20 percent are Christians (mostly Roman Catholic) and 5 percent Muslims. The literacy rate of Togo is still low. Elementary-school education is available, but not everyone takes advantage of the opportunity. Those who want a higher education go elsewhere, usually to France.

CITIES

Lomé, the capital, has a population of more than 100,000. Located directly on the Gulf of Guinea, it is also a deepwater port. Lomé is the most modern city in Togo and consequently also has the largest percentage of European residents.

Sokodé, about 200 miles (322 km) inland from the coast, is Togo's second largest city, its population a little more than 40,000.

A highway runs directly north from Lomé to Atakpamé, Sokodé, Lama-Kara, Sansanné-Mango, and Dapango. There are also many side roads, most of them unpaved. A railroad connects Lomé to Palimé, Atakpamé, and Blitta, and also extends eastward along the coast to Anécho, and an international airport at Lomé links Togo with other countries.

AGRICULTURE

About 90 percent of the people of Togo still work in agriculture. Most of the farming is for subsistence—the crops primarily cassava (manioc), yams, beans, sorghum, maize (corn), millet, and rice. The exports are small. Among them are coffee, cacao, palm kernels, cotton, and peanuts. Only the palm kernels come from native plants, the oil palms.

Togo is far from being a leader or even progressive in agriculture. Africa, for example, provides more than 60 percent of the world's cacao. Ghana, Togo's immediate neighbor to the west, exports large amounts of cacao, its total amounting to close to half of the world's supply. By comparison, Togo exports a mere fraction. Much more could be grown in Togo.

Cacao was introduced to Africa from the New World. Unusual for a plant, the cacao tree bears its flowers on "cush-

An outdoor market in Lomé, the capital of Togo.

ions" on its trunk and on large branches. Fertilized flowers then develop into football-shaped fruits, or pods, each containing a number of seeds that are embedded in a sweetish pulp. The seeds are fermented, then dried and roasted to make chocolate and cocoa. Cocoa "butter," the oily fat extracted from the seeds, is used in making soap.

Other agricultural opportunities are also available to Togo. Coffee, a native of Brazil, is grown in Togo now as it is elsewhere in Africa, but much more could be grown than at present. Togo could also do more processing of its basic food products before they leave the country. This would give the Togolese additional work while at the same time escalating the price they get for their products.

INDUSTRY

Togo's principal income is from the mining of phosphates that are used in making fertilizers and synthetics. Most of the phosphate mines are near Atakpamé. The country also has large limestone deposits, a resource now being utilized for a huge cement factory located near Lomé. Marble is also quarried, and there are small iron ore deposits and some diamonds.

HISTORY AND GOVERNMENT

The Europeans arrived off the Togo coast in the early 1400s, and through the 1600s and even later, the slave trade was active in the region. In the late 1800s, the area came under German control as a model colony called Togoland. After World War I, the German colony was broken into two portions by the League of Nations. One, which has since been absorbed by Ghana, was put under the administration of Great Britain. The other, which constitutes the Togo of today, became the charge of France in what was then French West Africa.

Togo was given its independence in 1960, and most of the years since then have been tumultuous. Togo is still an African country in which a political rally is signaled by the beat of the drum. The country is at present under a military rule and is headed by Major General Gnassingbe Eyadema. The relationship between Togo and its neighbors—Ghana and Benin—has so far not been especially friendly.

6
PEOPLE'S REPUBLIC OF BENIN

Three and a half million people live in this small country of 43,484 square miles (112,622 sq km), which is about the size and shape of the state of Tennessee, but long in a north-south direction. The narrow strip fronts on the Gulf of Guinea with a 78-mile (125-km) coastline and stretches northward for some 400 miles (620 km), its northern third only slightly wider than its coast.

A barrier of sandbars separates the low mangrove coast from battering by waves of the rough Gulf. Benin has no natural harbors or river mouths. Behind its sandy beaches, now popular with tourists, are lagoons, most of them with no outlet to the sea. The lagoons blend into the mangrove forests that change on higher land into dense tropical forests. Northward the land is hilly, some of the rises more than 1500 feet (457 m) in elevation. Then the country levels into a wooded plateau and finally savannahs. In the northwestern section are the Atakora Mountains that reach an elevation of 2400 feet (733 m).

The Niger River forms much of the country's northeastern border, but the longest river in the country is the Ouémé, which runs through the country for 285 miles (459 km) and with 125 miles (200 km) navigable by steamers. The Ouémé empties into the Gulf of Guinea at Porto-Novo. The Mono River, forming the boundary with Togo, is navigable from Para Nové to Grand-Popo, for some 50 miles (80 km), but is also subject to heavy flooding in the rainy season.

CLIMATE
Southern Benin is tropical—hot and humid, its average temperature is 82 degrees F (28 degrees C). Along the coast there are two wet seasons—one from March through July and another from September through November. Inland and to the north, rains come from May through September, the heaviest in July and August. During the long dry season from December through March, cool northeastern winds called harmattans blow steadily.

PEOPLE
For many years, Benin was called Dahomey; its name was changed in 1967. The old name came from the Dahomeans, or Fons, who have made up the largest portion of the region's population since ancient times. About 30 percent of Benin's population today are still Dahomeans.

In the early days, these tall, longheaded Negroes controlled the area by force. They maintained a well-trained army of more than 15,000, and about half of the warriors were women, noted as fierce fighters and exceptionally skilled at using weapons. These people were famed, too, for the decorative scars on their bodies, resulting from cuts made on them when they were young, usually just as they became young adults. The location, number, and design of the scars had special meaning.

About 10 percent of the people in Benin belong to the Adja tribe, which had a kingdom along the coast as early as 1100. Other native tribes include the Aizo (closely related to the Dahomeans), Bariba, Yoruba, Somba, and Fulani. Because of the great differences among the various tribes, particularly among those in southern and northern Benin, conflicts occurred in early times and, to a degree, still do. This has made it difficult for the people of Benin to act in unity as a nation.

About 65 percent of the people of Benin still follow their ancient tribal beliefs. Christians, most of whom are Roman Catholics, and Muslims are roughly equally divided, each accounting for more than 15 percent of the population. The mystic practice of voodoo was originated by the tribal people of Benin. It was carried from there by the slaves to the West Indies, where it has since flourished and is most strongly identified with the people of Haiti. The secret voodoo rituals, performed by a priest or priestess, took place in the darkness of night and were aimed at getting rid of an enemy by some violent destructive force. Filled with dread and superstition, a voodoo victim not uncommonly died.

The literacy rate in Benin is still only slightly more than 5 percent, but the educational system is being improved. Benin now boasts of having more students in its public schools than does any other nation that was once a territory of French West Africa. The educational system also includes technical schools for learning specific trades. The University of Benin, with more than 2000 students, is supported by France.

Because Benin was for a long time a part of French West

Africa, the country's official language is French, which is also taught in the schools. Most of the inhabitants speak in their native tribal languages, however. Among these are Fon, Yoruba, Bariba, and Fulani.

While Cotonou glitters with lights and has all the features and facilities of any modern city, the hinterland of Benin still reflects the old ways of life. Long ago the natives hunted the elephant for its ivory until it was nearly extinct, and they also hunted the buffalo and the antelope for food. Those who lived along the coast caught fish—and still do. They sell or trade their fish for vegetables and fruits that are grown by people from inland areas. But everywhere today, farming is by far the most important way of getting food.

Almost everyone has one or more fields. These are traditionally cleared by the men, then planted and harvested by the women. After the land no longer produces, it is allowed to go fallow, and new land is cleared. Corn (maize), yams, onions, peppers, peanuts, tomatoes, beans—these are among the common crops grown for local consumption. Among the fruits are pineapples, bananas, and papayas. Because of the warm climate, it is possible to get two or more crops per year.

A favorite native food is called akasan. First cornmeal is soaked in water until it begins to ferment. Then it is boiled until it is thick enough to mold into orange-sized balls. These are allowed to harden and then are eaten like bread, usually dipped into some sort of sauce.

People who live in the country cook most of their meals outdoors over open fires. Nearly all live in small clusters of houses, or villages, and a single residence also consists of several buildings around a central court that is enclosed by a wall of woven sticks known as a wattle. The wattles are generally plastered with mud. The walls of the houses are usually made in the same way.

The most distinctive pieces of furniture in the houses are stools. Those used by the men are generally elaborate and made from a single piece of wood. The stools used by the women are typically only a few inches tall and are carried with them wherever they go. The natives also carve statues, staffs, masks, and other objects. They make drums, horns, and rattles for musical instruments to accompany their singing and dancing.

CITIES

Porto-Novo, the capital, and *Cotonou,* its twin city, have a combined population of about 300,000. They are located on the Gulf of Guinea. Cotonou is the principal deepwater port, handling more than a million tons of cargo annually. Benin's 360 miles (580 km) of railroads are focused on Cotonou, one line extending the short distance eastward to Porto-Novo and then north to the town of Pobé. Another line goes west to Ouidah, then north to Abomey and Parakou. The railroad is owned and operated by the government.

Other towns are linked to Cotonou by the country's nearly 4000 miles (6436 km) of roads, about 10 percent of which are paved. The roads extend the full length of the country—to Malanville on the Niger River in the north. East-west roads in the south connect Benin with Togo to the west and Nigeria to the east.

A few miles outside of Cotonou is an international airport that keeps Benin in contact with other parts of the world. A smaller airline joins the city with Abomey, Kandi, Parakou, and other towns within the country.

NATURAL RESOURCES

In per capita income, which is less than $200 per year, Benin is extremely poor, but it has a wealth of natural resources that it has only begun to appreciate—its rich soil and its native plants and animals. Benin is poor in mineral resources, except for limestone and a low-grade iron ore.

With Niger and Upper Volta, Benin shares one of the most beautiful parks in all of Africa. Called "W" National Park, nearly half of its 2,800,000 acres (1,132,000 ha) are in Benin. It is located on the Niger River where the river's course makes a W-shaped bend. Nearby, too, Benin has still another park, the 640,000-acre (275,000-ha) Pendjari National Park, and there are nine smaller nature and hunting reserves. The total of parks and reserves in Benin is about 4½ million acres (2 million ha).

Of all the wildlife reserves in West Africa, the "W" National Park is considered by most authorities to be the most valuable. The area averages only 850 feet (259 m) above sea level, and much of it is in deep gorges cut by the Tapoa and Mékrou rivers. The Atakora Mountains stretch across the park, and there are also savannahs and semiarid lands that extend from Mauritania southward across Africa's hump. Because of the Niger's circuitous course through the area, water holes remain even through most of the dry season. In the rainy season, the lowlands are flooded. In addition to the thick grasses, there are many acacia trees plus gallery trees in the wetter areas.

Roans, hartebeests, and kobs roam the savannahs, while waterbucks, reedbucks, oribis, red-fronted gazelles, and sitatungas abound in the wetter areas. Duikers and topis are also found there, and everywhere there are elephants and water buffaloes as well as hippopotamuses in the rivers. In the forests

[53]

there are baboons, vervets, and red monkeys. Jackals, hyenas, and lions roam the park, and though less common, there are cheetahs, caracals, wildcats, and leopards, too. At floodtime on the rivers, the area is visited by numerous kinds of waterfowl, wading birds, and others, and there are pythons, turtles, crocodiles, and monitor lizards.

AGRICULTURE

Benin's economy is at present based almost wholly on agriculture, most of which is for self-subsistence. But the fertile soil could produce much greater amounts for export.

The land regularly yields large crops from the native oil palms, the country's major export being palm oil or palm kernels. Palm oil is also used in large amounts locally. The fruit of the African oil palm is similar to the coconut but is much smaller. The exported oil is used primarily in making soaps. Also exported are cotton, coffee, and cashew nuts, all of them growing steadily in importance.

GOVERNMENT

The Portuguese were the first Europeans to land on the coast of Benin. They established a trading post at what is now Porto-Novo. Later the brisk slave trade brought the French, British, Dutch, and Spaniards to the coast where they built forts that

A young farm worker in a cornfield
in Benin. Corn is one of the most
important crops in the country.

[55]

date to the 1600s and 1700s. For many years the tribes here fiercely resisted the French, even after a treaty was signed with the coastal-dwelling Adja in 1851. Benin, at the time called Dahomey, became a part of French West Africa in 1904. In August 1960, the nation was granted its independence.

Since 1960, there have been many internal struggles. The country is under the political and military rule of Colonel Mathieu Kerekou and an 11-man Council of the Revolution. Kerekou's rule is the sixth since Benin became a nation, and the nation remains unsettled.

7
REPUBLIC OF EQUATORIAL GUINEA

Smallest of the African countries, Equatorial Guinea contains only 10,830 square miles (28,051 sq km), making it about the size of the state of Maryland. Its population is estimated to be 300,000.

Equatorial Guinea is divided into two widely separated parcels of land, or provinces. The smaller of the two is Macías Nguema Biyogo, formerly known as Fernando Póo. A volcanic island of 785 square miles (2020 sq km), it is located in the Gulf of Guinea directly west of Cameroon. Included is the much smaller island of Pigalu, formerly Annobón.

Malabo (Santa Isabel), the capital, is located on Macías Nguema Biyogo. The island has short streams that cascade from the highlands. In the center of the island is Pico de Santa Isabel with an elevation of 1000 feet (3000 m). To the south is the lower Pico de Moka, and between the two is a valley.

To the south and east and located on the mainland is the

larger of the two provinces: Río Muni, with an area of 10,020 square miles (25,942 sq km). Off its coast are the small islands of Corisco, Elobey Chico, and Elobey Grande. Río Muni is bordered to the north by Cameroon and to the east and south by Gabon. It is essentially a jungle with a few mountain peaks. The main river is Río Benito, which is navigable for only about 7 miles (11 km). The river extends through the middle of the country. Río Muni has no natural harbor, its coast consisting of a long beach backed by low cliffs.

CLIMATE

For a brief period in winter between December and February, Equatorial Guinea has a dry season, but for the remainder of the year, there are heavy rains. The rainfall at Malabo averages 76 inches (193 cm), but it ranges to as much as 430 inches (109 cm) at Ureka. Both on Macías Nguema Biyogo and in Río Muni, the weather is described best as hot and muggy the year round. The temperature averages 80 degrees F (27 degrees C).

PEOPLE

Macías Nguema Biyogo is populated by the Bubi, who are of Bantu descent, plus Nigerians, and people from Sierra Leone. There is also a substantial population of people from the West Indies. In addition to their tribal language, some speak an English dialect. The official language is Spanish.

Nearly everyone living in Río Muni, except in the coastal cities, belongs to one of the tribal groups of Cameroon or Gabon, primarily the Fang. Equatorial Guinea is thus predominantly Black African. Most of the Europeans who once lived there have left the country, fewer than a thousand remaining.

The literacy rate is low, the religion mainly tribal. About 60 percent of the natives were once converted to Christianity, almost all Roman Catholic, but in recent years Christians have been persecuted and expelled from the country.

CITIES

Malabo, its population about 50,000, is not only the capital city but also the financial and cultural center for the small nation. Malabo is located on the outer rim of an old volcano, and it is the only natural harbor on the island of Macías Nguema Biyogo. Like many cities in Africa today, it is a contrast between modern architecture and ways of life and the poverty of the vast majority. Malabo has an international airport.

Bata is the major port city of Río Muni. It has a population of about 30,000.

South along Río Muni's coast are the smaller timber ports of Mbini (Río Benito) at the mouth of the Mbini River and also Puerto Iradie at the mouth of the Muni River.

Roads extend from Bata to the country's interior, which is mostly jungle with only a scattering of market and administrative villages and farmed clearings.

HISTORY AND GOVERNMENT

Equatorial Guinea was visited by the Portuguese in 1471, and the slave trade was active there in the 1500s and 1600s. In 1778, Equatorial Guinea became a Spanish colony. The British, with the consent of Spain, used the country as headquarters for their antislavery patrols in the early 1800s.

Immediately after achieving its independence in 1968, the new nation came under the rule of President Francisco Macías

Nguema, and in 1972, he appointed himself as president for life. He maintained this position only by exerting full military and police force. The tension between the government and the people was great, and internal uprisings occurred with regularity.

Some of the conflict in recent times has been with the Nigerians. Equatorial Guinea's only significant export, for example, has been cacao that is grown on some 1000 plantations on Macías Nguema Biyogo, and for many years, all of the work was done by Nigerians. When the workers complained of brutality, poor working conditions, and low wages, their demands were ignored, and a number of the Nigerians were killed by soldiers of Equatorial Guinea. The Nigerians took their workers—some 45,000—home and then threatened to invade and take over the little island.

Some of the native Equatorial Guineans also left the country to avoid being forced to work on the cacao plantations under nearly slave labor conditions for the government. It has been estimated that as many as a fourth of the Equatorial Guineans are now living in self-imposed exile, mostly in Cameroon, Gabon, Nigeria, and Spain.

Coffee is grown in Río Muni, but only a small amount is exported. The production has been decreasing, in fact. Small amounts of palm kernels are also exported. Some timber is sold, but the industry has suffered from lack of financial support by Europeans.

The nation has continued on a downhill course toward bankruptcy. There are constant and critical shortages of food and other essentials, and the only citizens who get regular pay and who live in reasonable comfort are the soldiers and members of the police force. Even communications between Malabo and Río Muni are erratic.

Among African nations, Equatorial Guinea ranks as one of the poorest and most militant. Its atrocities (an estimated 12 percent of Equatorial Guineans have been slain) have been condemned by human rights organizations around the world. Equatorial Guinea is not an example of the sort of freedom and democracy aspired to by most Africans.

Several years ago, President Macías Nguema left Malabo and took the country's meager treasures with him. For a while he continued his rule from Bata in Río Muni, and then he hid deep in the jungle. Late in September 1979, he was hunted down and executed by his own cousin, who was also the country's chief security officer. The nation is now in the process of rebuilding, and the needed aid, both money and personnel, is coming from Spain.

FOR FURTHER READING

Africa South of the Sahara. London: Europa Publications, 1977.

Chinweizu. *The West and the Rest of Us*. New York: Random House, 1975.

Coughlan, Robert. *Tropical Africa*. New York: Time, 1962.

Davidson, Basil. *A Guide to African History*. New York: Double-day, Zenith Books, 1965.

Sachs, Moske, ed. *Africa—Worldmark Encyclopedia of the Na-tions*. 5th ed. New York: John Wiley and Sons, 1976.

Synge, Richard (ed.). *Africa Guide*. Essex, England: Africa Guide Company, 1976.

INDEX